THE

BLACK BOOK

OF

CARMARTHEN

Introduction
and
translations
by
MEIRION PENNAR

Artwork
by
JAMES NEGUS

Welsh diplomatic* text
by
J. GWENOGVRYN EVANS

*Diplomatic text, i.e., a printed letter-for-letter, word-for-word copy of the manuscript. Capital letters printed from type made from tracings of the originals.

Carmarthen Castle

the Black Book of Carmarthen

I Gwri

CONTENTS

guydi·taliessin·brthaud
kyssredin·vydawgan
Breudiud auelun nemhw *Breudd*
ur·y seeluir aedehoglho·
Hyrmrerhur y reuir·uir
guibir ar nuygelho·Guerthred
llara lywiau niuer nidhoffer
meuirer bru·Heur uim y dan
un dired abun dec liu guanec
gu·Hid·aur llauur uerh din
da·ae wffa arnuy dalho·Gua
ech·

THE BLACK BOOK

As the name already indicates, The Black Book of Carmarthen has traditionally been connected with the ancient town of Carmarthen. It has been said to have been produced by one of the Welsh-speaking monks of the Augustinian Priory of St. Johns in Carmarthen who was a bit of an amateur in the art of copying, but loved Welsh literature and wanted to anthologise poems with a Dyfed if not Carmarthen bias. He may have had to do this in an institution the members of which would have looked askance at his labour of love. What, Taffy, are you doing there? For the other monks were probably Normans and English. But then Welsh persons have had to further their beloved culture in alien institutional surroundings since then. Our Austin canon smiled and said, 'Ah' and went on copying. All we can say is that we are deeply grateful to him. Certain poems would never have survived if it were not for him. Nor would the graphic wonder of the Black Book be with us today. It may be amateurish, a bit of a manuscriptual mess according to the connoisseur, what with differing scripts and letter sizes, but it is a feast to the eye, and certainly a literary beano.

Doubt has been thrown on the connection with Carmarthen. But why the book be given on conjecture to say Whitland when the only place it has been linked with is Carmarthen? When tradition has it and we have no proof otherwise then from Carmarthen it comes. Sir John Price of Brecon who did a lot of work collecting manuscripts at the time of the Dissolution said that it came from the Priory there. It got a black cover eventually and hence the name. Its contents too indicate strongly that the anthologist

St. Peter's Church, Carmarthen.

was from the area. The fact that the central portion of the manuscript is given up to long poems in the *persona* of Myrddin corroborates the Carmarthen link. The legend of Myrddin is said to be in part a fictional explanation of the name of the town. Of course he may simply have come from Carmarthen. We know that the name of Caerfyrddin is derived from the Roman name of the fortress, Moridunum. Myrddin as poet and prophet was known in Wales as early as the tenth century, for he is referred to in the prophetic poem Armes Prydain which was composed by a staunch supporter of the dynasty of Deheubarth (South-West Wales). The connection made between Myrddin, a poet from Northern Britain and a contemporary of Taliesin, and the town of Carmarthen was made at least as early as the time of the composition of Armes Prydain. There are numerous references to places in Dyfed in the Myrddin poems in the Black Book of Carmarthen and they reveal a striking and emotional loyalty to the Southern dynasty of Deheubarth.

Dating the book is not without its problems, but it is generally accepted that it was produced around 1250. But a lot of material in it is far older than that. For our understanding of it we owe much to A. O. H. Jarman.

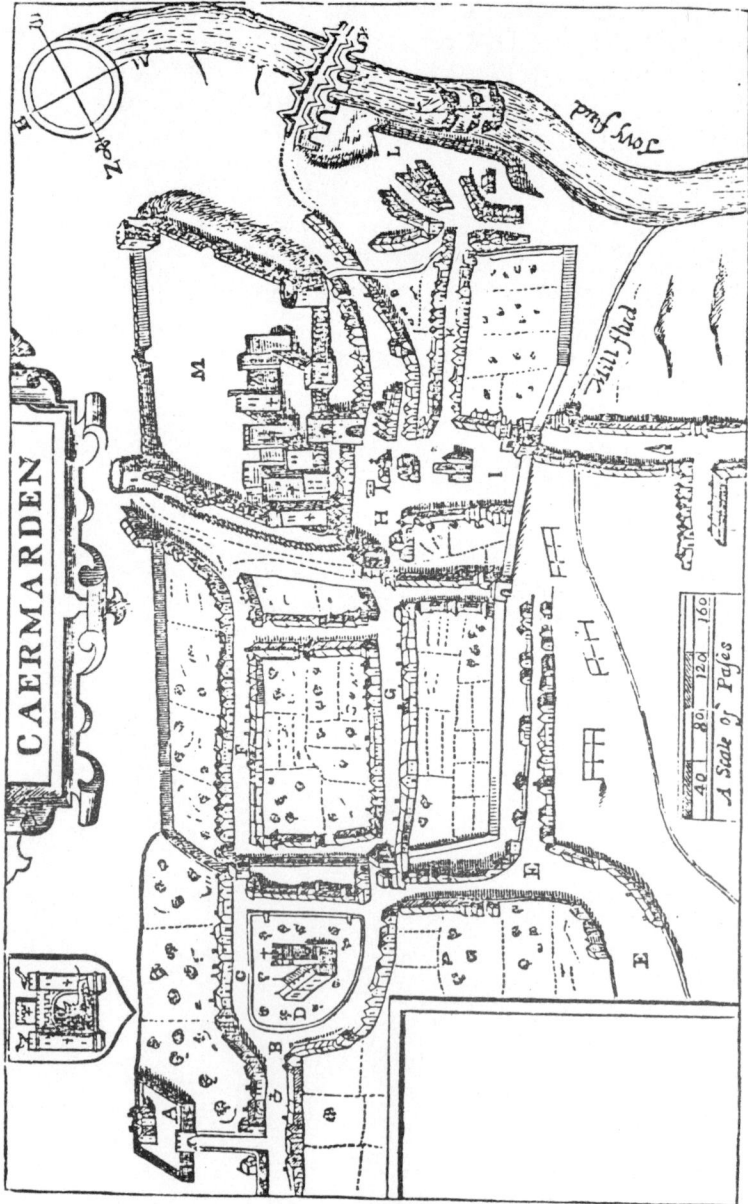

Map of Carmarthen, after Speed (1610).

One gets the feeling that the copyist regarded the poems ostensibly by Myrddin as the centre-piece of his collection. But he was drawn naturally to the poems produced by the monastic tradition of Wales. These chiselled gems figure at the beginning of the book, preceded only by the conversation of Myrddin and Taliesin, and may originally have been set in position there in order to salve the middle legendary section before his conscience, his friends, and his God. He intersperses a few later on amongst material inspired by lore and legend. There are also one or two praise poems. The one to Hywel ap Goronwy who died in 1106 shows the local Deheubarthian bias very clearly. The poems by Cynddelw to Madog ap Maredudd, a Powys chieftain, are a little more puzzling. But Cynddelw was a famous poet of the twelfth century who praised the princely families throughout the whole of Wales. There was a link through marriage between the dynasty of Deheubarth and Powys, for Rhys ap Gruffydd took as wife the daughter of Madog. What is rather odd is that the Carmarthen monk didn't get round to copying poems addressed to Lord Rhys himself, or to his sons. Maybe at the time of copying the hold of Llywelyn on Carmarthen made the inclusion of any poems to that family risky. After that, the town was in English hands, from 1223 onwards, and any honourable mention of the rightful owners of Deheubarth in a book compiled within the town would have been taboo.

The religious poems are very special. According to Geraint Gruffydd they may well have been composed by the same person, blessed with an intense devotional piety, around the middle of the twelfth century, at a time of religious renewal within the Church. They seem to belong to the tradition in Celtic lands of hermit poetry - incandescent pieces created out in the open, in the God-created wild, much like their counterparts in Ireland. The Celts were among the first to fall in love with the earth, God-given, and even in its wildest retreats, never godforsaken. Not Nature, so much as the Creation, the earth lying at its heart. We find this love expressed at its most obfuscating in the poems of Dafydd ap Gwilym later on. But the lover of retreats, leafy nooks, starry nights, existed in Wales long before either Romantic or Troubadour or even Wandering Cleric. Of Maytime. Of Cuckoos. In Ireland they were called Culdees.

Maytime is the nicest time,
birds are loud,
trees are green;
ploughs are in the furrow,
oxen in the yoke.
The sea is green,
lands have many colours.

To love the earth is no sin, for God gave it. God gave love for women too, but for a Culdee this must be foresworn. The conflict between the religious and secular, between the otherworldly and the earthly, is not better characterised than in the poem entitled 'I had a dream last night,' where the rather damp, if not wet, nature of the dream the poet has is steamed off by the iron of proverbial wisdom and religious fervour:

I had a dream last night:
cute
would be its interpreter.

12

One may not relate
its naughtiness:
who has not seen it
will not know...
    leading a host
    is a fine thing;
    a locality's cowardice
    doesn't make for pride...
I was under the same coverlet
as a fair maiden
of the hue of the wave
among the pebbles...

In order to blunt the erotic allure of the lines, he comically sticks a proverb or two between the talk about the dream and the revelation of its content: 'leading a host is a fine thing.' There must have originally been much more about the dream. But our monk says, 'No more,' and the rest of the poem is a series of proverbs put into verse. The dream poem is like certain poems that Dafydd ap Gwilym and the 'clêr' or popular clerical poets of the mediaeval period wrote considerably later. It shows that the sensual clerical muse of Europe so much at variance with the traditional morality of the Church and which is to be found most gloriously in the collection called the Carmina Burana put to music by Carl Orff existed in Wales a long time before Dafydd ap Gwilym.

The poem entitled 'Praising God' is in the tradition of the poetry of self-denial and remorse common in mediaeval Wales and Europe. *Diofryd* in Welsh meant an oath not to indulge in worldly and fleshly pleasures. Listen to the Welshman still caressing the beloved things of his sinful past, while bidding farewell to them:

13

After horses
and drinking new mead,
feasting,
making love to women,
I don't sleep,
I think...

He thinks about his end. Death is the great
leveller and lurks outside the door. Your body
goes into decline in a land where joy is clouded:

we are in a land
where pleasaunce
is troubled...
like leaves,
we,
from the tip
of withered trees.

The *drud* or foolhardy one does not tremble. He
has no notion of earthly time and duty and therefore has no inkling of eternal life:

He doesn't get up early,
he doesn't greet you,
he doesn't stay put,
he doesn't chant a prayer...

Old-age, inevitable and wrinkled, has a melan-
choly tenderness which only a darling man could
express:

hearing
sight
bite
fade
away...

The poems 'Praising God' and 'To the Trinity' have an inevitability that is totally convincing whether you are religious or not. Everything created praises God. The Celtic passion for the creation is again so apparent here:

male and female,
seven days and stars blessed you,
air and atmosphere blessed you,
books and letters blessed you...

Again the Trinity is the triple creator, a throwback to the veneration of the triple deities so beloved of the Celts, and the spawners of life and land:

who is three together,
who is God himself;
the one who made
Tuesdays and Mondays
man and woman...

Yet the intellect of the man is charged with heart-felt love for life. There seems to be a learned scientism coupled with a sense of wonder: God has a divine energy but is the maker of opposites, a mind-boggling creativity. There is such tenderness in his God who made:

a letter in wax
flame in a wick
love in sensibility,
and a maiden,
beloved, gentle...

The poem to Maytime already alluded to has a stupendous vision of God the inescapable, all-penetrating, loving pursuer. Cuckoos in spring make longing well up. He thinks of the dear ones he has lost; but then he says that no place in the world is too far-flung and too wild that it can elude God. Sinful man cannot evade his judgment and grace. Grieving man will be comforted.

On hill,
in hollow,
on islands in the sea,
everywhere you go
before blessed Christ
there is no place that is God-forsaken.

The hermit of the wilderness then projects his love of isolation and solitude into heavenly bliss. Heaven is *alltudedd* (exile) and also otherworldliness. But all are together there. There is no separation:

Amongst your people
Christ
I mayn't be sad.

This incredible poem juxtaposes earthly loss and heavenly restoration in a purgatorial journey laced with love and tears:

with Christ the blessed
dread
they do not suffer.

It is astounding how this monk took to the hermit in our literature. For the Myrddin poems are those of an outcast, a lonely man, condemned by circumstance to live in the wilderness. Such loneliness struck a chord in his monastic soul, lover of retreat and solitude. Maybe he felt that he was an outlaw in his own country, a Welshman

16

in Norman Carmarthen, isolated by his love for his own language. He was also experiencing the wilderness, the wild berries of God's grace being the succulent poems he was copying. He was on his own in his Welsh poems. In the poems spoken by Myrddin the tragedy of the Deheubarthian overshadowed by Gwynedd on the one hand and English and Normans on the other was eked out. The compiler underwent certain catharsis while fondly copying the tortured words of Myrddin.

Merlin is big. Everywhere. And here we have in the Black Book of Carmarthen the core of the Merlin legend which in varying forms has captivated the whole of the world. Let's call him Myrddin. Merlinus was Geoffrey of Monmouth's very considerable attempt to make the Welsh combination of 'rdd' easier to pronounce for all who were not Welsh. But if you can say Carmarthen, then you will have no difficulty in saying Myrthin.

We usually connect Myrddin with Arthur. The first stage along this road was effected by Geoffrey of Monmouth because, in his History of the Kings of Britain (1136), he identified Merlinus with Ambrosius who told Voltigern why his tower in Snowdonia collapsed. The connection with Carmarthen and the Southern Kingdom of Deheubarth may have a more substantial basis than we thought. For if we look carefully at the first poem in the Black Book, the conversation between Myrddin and Taliesin, we find the two bards and prophets talking about the king of the southern dynasty, Elgan, being defeated and killed at the hands of Maelgwn Gwynedd from North Wales. This battle is then linked with the battle of Arfderydd in the North of Britain. Elgan was a des-

17

cendant of Dyfnwal while Maelgwn was descended from Coel. We know that these two dynasties were rivals in the North of Britain also. Rhydderch, one of the protagonists of the battle of Arfderydd in Cumbria, with which the tragic Myrddin is intimately connected, belonged to the dynasty of Dyfnwal and Gwenddolau, his opponent was a descendant of Coel. In other words the two battles were fought between the same two rival factions. Indeed certain lines seem to suggest that Arfderydd was fought because of the bitterness engendered by the slaying of Elgan by Maelgwn. Rhydderch in fact avenged the death of Elgan by defeating Gwenddolau (whose name is preserved in Carwinelow near Arthuret, derived from Caer Wenddolau). Contrary to recent argument, the sons of Eliffer mentioned in the poem were on Gwenddolau's side.

Maelgwn's host came keenly.
Warriors of strident battle
bloody
of the battle of Arfderydd
this is the cause.

No wonder therefore that the sixteenth century poet Tudur Aled when writing a poem pleading with two rival factions within a certain family in Noth East Wales should refer to the sheer futility of the battle of Arfderydd.

If the conversation between Myrddin and Taliesin belongs to the eleventh century, then the *Afallennau* (Appletrees, so-called because each stanza begins with the word *afallen* [appletree]) are in their original form much earlier, for in them is the core of the Myrddin legend. The *Afallennau* must have formed the poetic monologues in the

18

ancient saga of Myrddin where the prose portions have been lost as in the saga of Heledd or Llywarch Hen. Since these have their roots in the ninth century, maybe the Myrddin story belongs to the same period. But the *Afallennau* as we have them have been reworked and updated up to the time of the copier. For the original Myrddin we must go back to the sixth century in Northern Britain. With Taliesin, Urien, Rhydderch and Gwallawg. To Penrith and beyond.

The *Afallennau* give us a couple of clues as to the story of Myrddin as it is developed in the early stages from the sixth century onwards. For the original tale is half-hidden among the prophecies which belong to a later period. It is obvious that Myrddin hides in the apple-tree in some solitary neck of the woods of Celyddon, away from the wrath of Rhydderch.

Sweet apple-tree
that in Llanerch grows,
its mystique
will hide it
from Rhydderch the king.

A certain Gwenddydd is mentioned, who now no longer has regard for him. Gwasawg, who is Rhydderch's protector, is hell-bent on Myrddin's destruction. This is because Myrddin has 'destroyed' his son and daughter. He was at the battle of Arfderydd wearing a golden torque, indicating that he took part in the battle.

...now Gwenddydd doesn't love me,
doesn't greet me.
I am hated by Gwasawg,
Rhydderch's protector:

I brought about the ruin
of his son and daughter.

We read on and find that his lord Gwenddolau
has been killed, that Myrddin has the blood of
Gwenddydd's son on his hands.

O Jesus,
would that my end had come,
before coming on my hand
the blood of the son
of Gwenddydd.

As a result of all this, Myrddin loses his reason
and retreats to the forest of Celyddon with the
wild ones *(gwyllon)*. He has been there he says
for fifty years, suffering illness and longing, living
off apples and other fruits.

no steward can make it
to its glistening fruit.

In his state of exalted madness Myrddin prophesies it seems with the aid of a certain Chwyfleian
(White phantom):

Chwyfleian prophesies,
she tells a tale...

Thus the *Afallennau.* We know that an actual
battle took place at Arfderydd or modern-day
Arthuret near Longtown in Cumbria in 573. The
actual protagonists in this battle is still a matter
of argument, but Gwenddolau, Myrddin's lord in
the poem, was certainly killed there. Rhydderch,
whom Myrddin fears in the poem, was a glittering
chief famed for his generosity, but there is no
early record of his involvement in the battle. He

20

may have been the lord of Alclud (Strathclyde). Scholars like Rachel Bromwich and Molly Miller have argued that the battle was between two rival branches of the descendants of Coel, between Gwenddolau and the sons of Eliffer, Gwrgi and Peredur. There is evidence that the latter took part in the battle. Perhaps we should accept the Myrddin poems in the Black Book of Carmarthen as evidence that Rhydderch did in fact take part in the battle of Arfderydd. The Gwasawg mentioned in the poem as Rhydderch's protector is unknown.

The question as to whether Myrddin existed also arises. Was he perhaps the poet of Gwenddolau who, as Rachel Bromwich suggests, wrote the following lines of an elegy to his lord, preserved in one of the verses of the *Oianau:*

I saw Gwenddolau
a powerful king
gathering booty
far and wide.
Under my red earth
is he now
all quiet like,
the greatest
king of the north,
the greatest too
in tenderness.

Like the elegy to Geraint, this may be a dramatic piece recited by Myrddin in a saga about him and the battle of Arfderydd, but I think that Rachel Bromwich may well indeed have discovered an original Myrddin poem to be placed alongside the poems of Taliesin and Aneurin. The hallmarks of that early art are there.

21

The intriguing thing is that Nennius does not name him in his famous passage in the *Historia Britonum* (History of the Britons) in the tenth century. Aneurin and Taliesin are named, and others, but not Myrddin. Still, this does not prove that he did not exist. The tenth-century prophetic poem *Armes Prydain* refers to Myrddin as one who was known to have foretold the future. In the conversation between Myrddin and Taliesin we find Myrddin prophesying the battle of Arfderydd. Myrddin may well have been a native of Carmarthen, hence his name. Like Taliesin, who hailed from Powys, Myrddin moved up north, drawn to Cumbria by the fact that Gwenddolau the lord of the area around Longtown was, like Myrddin himself, a member of the dynasty of Coel. Myrddin may have been before then in the employ of members of the rival dynasty in South Wales.

In the *Cyfoesi*, another poem featuring Myrddin to be found in the Red Book of Hergest, the poet has another name, *llallogan*. A.O.H. Jarman, who has studied the Myrddin story extensively, links *llallogan* with the wild man called Lailoken in the legend of St. Kentigern. According to that scholar *Llallogan* was a Northern British wild man whose story came south, and who then became known as Myrddin. It may well be, however, that *Myrddin llallogan* of the Cyfoesi corresponded to *Myrddin Wyllt* of the Welsh Triads and was in fact the name of Myrddin in the wild. *Llallogan* can be interpreted to mean 'other, different, estranged.'

The *Cyfoesi* of the Red Book throws welcome light on the character of Gwenddydd mentioned in the poems in the Black Book. She is his sister *(chwaer)* in the Dialogue. She asks him questions

22

about the future which he answers, some of the events foretold corresponding to those prophesied in the Black Book poems. Thus Myrddin is guilty of killing his nephew. There is a tradition preserved in the *Vita Merlini* of Geoffrey of Monmouth that Rhydderch was married to Merlin's sister. The tragedy of Myrddin is now clear. By supporting the cause of Gwenddolau he was opposed to his own sister and perhaps killed her son during the course of the battle of Arfderydd. No wonder Myrddin became insane. In the *Cyfoesi* there is no enmity between Myrddin and Gwenddydd, which may mean that there were other versions of the story, but then Gwenddydd may well have visited Myrddin in his wild and deranged state, for they both were fascinated by future events.

The original mad Myrddin must have foretold events ensuing from the Arfderydd disaster. But in the poems in the Black Book we find him prophesying happenings which were to occur in the twelfth and thirteenth centuries, thus giving us clues as to when the verses were finally composed. In the *Afallennau* we have a possible reference to Rhys ap Gruffudd of Deheubarth, a twelfth-century prince, in the lines:

A young lad will arise
in the territory of the South.

We know that these following lines were inserted at the end of the second stanza, and are a reference to the ever-growing power of Llywelyn the Great, king of Gwynedd, and who called himself 'arglwydd Eryri' (lord of Snowdon):

and all around the reaper

23

English to the sickle put
by the venomous bile
of the lord of Eryri.

That same stanza has a possible reference to
the conquest of Eastern Powys by Penda as de-
picted so movingly in the poetry of the Heledd
saga elsewhere. The third stanza has a possible
reference to the early struggles between the Picts
and Scots. Stanzas eight and nine refer to the
vague eternal messianic Cadwaladr, a favourite,
with Arthur and Owain, for the poets of prophesy
in Wales, who will rid the Welsh of the Normans
and the English. The poem ends on a high note:

The Welsh will win,
glorious shall their dragon be.

Or put with fervour and aggression earlier on:

...giving the English
a hammering,
playing football
with their heads.

The *Oianau* or the Ohs of Myrddin, so-called
because each stanza begins with *oian* (oh), are
thought to be imitations of the *Afallennau*, picking
up the opening line from stanza four in that
poem. I wonder. It must have been another
series of stanzas from the original saga. The first
stanza retains the doubted tradition that Rhydderch in defeating pagan Gwenddolau was also fur-
thering the cause of Christianity. Myrddin tells
his beloved piglet to beware of Rhydderch:

...forage in the hidden place
in Argoedydd

24

away from fierce
Rhydderch the generous,
the tiller-man of the faith..

Also stanzas eight, nine and ten are from the original *cyfarwyddyd* or saga. Here is Myrddin deprived and threadbare, wintering in the forest with icicles in his hair. There are others. But much of the *Oianau* deal with the aspirations of the Welsh in the struggle with the Normans and the English. There are veiled references to the sons of Owain Gwynedd (stanza six), definite references to the wars of Llywelyn the Great, against the Prince of Powys (stanza eleven), between Llywelyn and King John (stanza seven) and to campaigns waged by the princes of Deheubarth around the same time (stanza twelve).

The Apple-tree poems make the most of the contrast between Myrddin now and Myrddin of yesteryear, a much loved theme in the literature of Celtic lands.

Sweet apple-tree
that grows beyond the Rhun...
at its base
I had fought
for a maiden's bliss
with shield on shoulder
and sword on hip,
and I myself slept
in the forest of Celyddon.

The same place, but a different Myrddin. Once a virile warrior fighting 'for a maiden's bliss' now a raving insomniac:

Ten years and two score

25

have I been
moving along
through twenty bouts of madness
with wild ones
in the wild...

He longs for peace everlasting, and here the poetry of the wild man and the wandering hermit become one:

After suffering illness
and longing
around the forest of Celyddon,
let me be
a blissful hireling
with the lord of hosts.

He suffers the contortions of guilt, another characteristic of the early Welsh saga, as in the story of Heledd, Llywarch Hen and Ysgolan. Personal guilt is very often compounded with general loss. Heledd bemoans the death of her brother Cynddylan and the devastation of Powys. Myrddin bewails the death of Gwenddolau and the loss of his kingdom. Heledd feels responsible for her brother's death, Myrddin feels guilty of the death of his sister's son. Actually, there is no hard evidence, in the Myrddin poems, that Myrddin actually killed his nephew, but like Heledd, he may have felt responsible because of his partisan involvement in the whole struggle.

O Jesus
would that my end had come,
before coming on my hand
the blood of the son
of Gwenddydd.

The Welsh were great exponents of the literature of loss. They were well acquainted with recurrent calamities. What with vain struggles with the Saxons on different fronts, with the Normans and then the English, our history has been etched with pain. We produced our myths to deal with it. Our fate was put down to divisiveness, to sin. Gildas started a long tradition of Judaic self-castigation. In our literature we find guilty parties involved in huge events leading to our constant harrowed erosion. The Battle of Arfderydd is one of these. There is a tradition about that battle, that it was fought for the puniest of reasons, that it started because of a quarrel between two shepherds as to who was to have a lark's nest. It became, with the battle of Camlan, the symbol of futile internecine strife amongst the Welsh throughout the ages, which made for weakness in the face of the foe. Myrddin was guilty of the ruination of a number of his nearest and dearest. But also of general woe:

Death took everybody away...

Small wonder then that Myrddin should also be made to voice the desire of reparation, of success, in the future.

Before the youth like the sun
with daring ways
will the English
be uprooted
and bards flourish.

In the *Afallennau* Myrddin invokes the otherworldly power of each apple-tree in turn, in order to overturn our history of loss, and herald a time when

The Brython's morale will be high,
the horns of celebration
will be blown,
the song
of peace,
of prosperity.

The realisation of this came, according to the
Black Book, using prophesy as hindsight, in the
time of Llywelyn the Great.

The *Oianau* gives a picture of Myrddin which
sears the heart. It is not here a matter of invo-
cation but a great outpouring to a grunting friend.
Pigs in Wales were revered and loved. They came
from Annwn or the Otherworld. Myrddin's prophesies the pig most certainly understood. The lin-
gering death of a people is here enshrined as well
as the terrible weight of the hours on an inmate
of the Forest of Celyddon:

Oh little piglet,
see the light of day,
listen to the call of the water-fowl,
shrill cries,
years
stretch out before us,
long
days...

Gain is prised out of disaster. He would not
wish the pain of survival on his snuffling com-
panion:

Oh little piglet,
oh of ohs,

in dire straits,
for God would cause setbacks,
is any bacon saved:
let that lot be mine -
let *her*
go for the sleep
of death.

The high dialectic contrast between the revelling
Christian Rhydderch and the ecstatic starveling
Myrddin is one of the indelible impressions left
on us by the Ohs:

Rhydderch the Generous
at his carousel,
little does he know tonight
the extent
last night
of my insomnia.
Snow to my thighs
surrounded by dingoes,
icicles in my hair,
my glory gone.

Escape from the terror of Rhydderch and his
'clever hounds' becomes, through the alchemy of
time and failure, the sheer relief of respite from
the onslaughts of the English.   The internecine
North has travelled to beleaguered Wales.

Oh little piglet,
it's so strange
that no second is like another.
The sound of the English
is now so far away -
that fundament of strife.

We are a 'people of affliction' and the Myrddin

poems are a map of that affliction and a guide to our future, good or bad. A huge myth which grew with us over the centuries. Our Cadwaladr, our Arthur, our saviour we searched in every age for him after the fall of Llywelyn the Last. To drive the English back into the brine whence they came, or to reinstate Brythonic authority over Britain. It was Owain Lawgoch, then Glyndŵr. The more unlikely William Herbert, that powerful Yorkist who finally drove the Lancastrians from their last stronghold in Harlech in 1468. Then Henry Tudor. At last we thought we had found our Arthur. Henry Tudor called his son Arthur, and prepared the way for Henry VIII to 'annexe' Wales officially. And Myrddin still foretells

that the Brythons
will have the measure of the English.

There is an intensity to the Ohs that makes for a sweeping vista of a total restoration, 'the endowment of triumph' as the poet puts it, or the hallucinations of utter decadence worthy of a Bosch:

and evil kings
like rotting fruit:
and bishops harbouring
no-good raiders of churches;
monks fully deserving
their burden of sin.

The world will become topsy-turvy. A common scenario in mediaeval literature. But here it is lent a poignancy that only the subjugated people can know, and mordent satire is mingled with guilt:

I do prophesy
to world's end
women without shame
men without bravery.

There are other treasures. The grave stanzas
are antiquarian and elegaic pieces mourning
ancient heroes, and belong to the tenth century.
The Geraint poems, probably ninth century, again
reveal the marvel of Celtic repetitive art within
a saga about the death of that Devon king fighting
against his enemies at the battle of Langport, on
the river Parret in Somerset. The elegy juxtaposes the loss of Geraint with his former glory,
astride his magnificent horses. Thanks to that
Austin canon for culling such riches.

WELSH TEXT AND TRANSLATIONS

The following selected passages from the Black Book are presented with the Welsh text followed by an English translation.   The extract below, from the version of the Black Book by J.G. Evans, is given to clarify the methods he used in making a printed version of the Welsh text of the manuscript: "The present text has been reproduced diplomatically, line for line, character for character, space for space.   Every letter which the writer failed to read easily is faintly underdotted; every letter retraced has a wavy line under it; and every letter become illegible through effacement, or damage to the vellum is underlined. Different sizes of types are used for the different sizes of handwriting of the manuscripts.   Most of the large initials are traced copies of the originals.   The greater number of these are coloured red, a good many are green, and a few are chrome, the prevailing colour used for patching the smaller capitals represented by heavier faced type. These capitals are of all sizes, and in a variety of styles, involving the use of fourteen distinct founts on different sized bodies... I believe that only my assistant (Mr. George Jones of Lampeter) and myself have ever attempted such a combination of founts, and that the Black Book of Carmarthen is unique among printed books.   It is to all intents and purposes a facsimile in characters which all can read.   No pains have been spared to make the readings faithful and reliable transcripts of the original..."

Myrtin

Moz truan gen⁄

hyᶠ moz truan.

aderẏv. amke⁄

duẏv a chaᵈuan. Oed lla⁄

chaʀ kẏulauaʀ kẏula⁄ 5

uan. Oed ẏſcuid o trẏu⁄

ʀuẏd o tʀẏuan. **Talẏes**.

Oed maelgun a uelun

in imuan ẏ teulu rac toz⁄

ẏuulu nẏthauant . Myrtin.

Rac deuur ineutuʀ ẏ tirr⁄
an . Rac eʀʀith . agurrith
ẏ aʀ Welugan . Mein wi⁄
nev indiheu adẏgan . Mo⁄
ch guelheʀẏ niueʀ gan el⁄
gan . Och oe leith maur a⁄
teith ẏ deuthan . Taliessin.

Rẏs undant oet ʀẏchv⁄

ant ẏ taʀian . hid attad ẏ
daeth rad kẏulaun . llaſ
kẏnduʀ tra meſſur ẏ ku⁄
ẏnan . llas haelon o din⁄
on tra uuan . Ŏʀẏuiʀ .
nod mauʀ eu clod. gan.
elgan .Ŏiʀtín. ŎRuẏ a th⁄
rui . Ruẏ . aʀuẏ . trav a th⁄
rau imdoeth ẏ doethan .

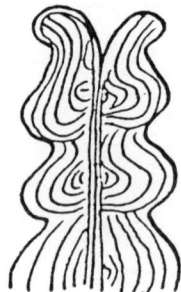

brau amelgan . llat dẏ
uel oe diuet kẏulauan
ab erbin ae ueʀin aw
Calieṡ naethant ILu maelgun
bu ẏſcun ẏ doethan . aeʀ
wiʀ kad trẏbelidiad .
guaedlan . Neu gueith
aʀẏwdeʀit pan vit ẏ
deunit . o hid ẏ wuchit

ẏ darpan . llẏa̋s peleidrad

guaedlad guadlan . llẏ⁄

aus . aᴇʀwiʀ bʀẏv bre⁄

uaul vidan . ILẏaus

ban bʀiv heʀ . llẏaus

ban fohᴇʀ . llẏauſ ev

hẏmchuel in eu hẏmv⁄

an . **Talieſſin** Seith me⁄

ib eliffeʀ . Seith guiʀ

ban brouheʀ. Seith guaew nẏ
ochel in eu feithran . 𝕸𝖞𝖗𝖙𝖎𝖓 .
Seith tan. vueliɴ. Seith kad
kẏueʀbin . Seithued kinve⁄
liɴ ẏ pop kinhuan . 𝕮𝖆𝖑𝖎𝖊𝖘𝖘𝖎𝖓 .
Seith guaew gowanon. Seith
loneid awon . O guaed kinre⁄
inon ẏ dẏlanuan . 𝕸𝖞𝖗𝖙𝖎𝖓 .
Seith ugein haelon . aaethan
ẏgwllon . ẏg coed keliton . ẏ .
daʀuuan . Can ẏf mi mẏʀtin
guẏdi. talieffin . bithaud . .c.
kẏffrediɴ . vẏ darogan .

MYRDDIN CONVERSES WITH TALIESIN

Myrddin:
So sad am I,
so sad,
at what happened to Cedfyw and Cadfan.
The noise of the battle was shrill:
shields were stained,
pierced through.

Taliesin:
I could see Maelgwn fighting.
His retinue are not mute
before the huge host.

Myrddin:
They are mustering
in two hosts
before two men:
before Errith and Gwrrith
on White Boy.
They will surely bring
Bay Lad.
Soon the host of Elgan may be seen,
O the long journey made because of his death.

Taliesin:
Rhys One-Tooth whose shield's span
was a wonder
has come to you
with ample bounty.
Cyndur was slain
whose lament for him
was beyond measure.
Men who were generous
while they lived
were killed, with Elgan,
three men,
conspicuous,
of great renown.

Myrddin:

They came thick and strong,
more and more,
hither and thither
came terror to me
for Elgan's sake.
In his last battle
Dywel ab Erbin and his men
did they kill.

Taliesin:

Maelgwn's host came keenly.
Warriors of strident battle,
bloody,
of the battle of Arfderydd
this is the cause:
all their lives along
they have been getting ready.

Myrddin:

Host of raucous, blood-spurting strife;
host of warriors,
broken
they shall be,
exterminated;
host to be bruised,
host to be put to flight,
host to retreat
in the midst of fighting.

Taliesin:

The seven sons of Eliffer,
seven men
put to the test,
seven spears
that will not waver
in their seven destinies.

Myrddin:

Seven sparking fires,
seven Cynfelins
in the van of every battle.

Taliesin:
Seven spears of Gofannon,
seven riverfuls of might,
they ooze
with the blood of chieftains.
Myrddin:
Mad
have gone seven score
of the generous.
They ended their days
in Coed Celyddon.
For I,
Merlin,
as Taliesin before me,
shall see my prophesy
go far and wide.

Breuduid a uelun neithw⁄
ir. ẏſceluit ae dehoglho .
Nẏ ritreithir ẏ reuit . niſ
guibit aʀ nuẏgelho . Gueithred
llara llẏuiau niuer nid hoffet
meiuret bro . Neur uum ẏdan
un duted a bun dec liu guanec
gro . Nid cur llauur uʀth din
da . ae coffa arnuẏdalho . Gua⁄

eth.

vẏgniw odiuattep . ir nep nuẏ⁄
hatnappo . Nẏtiuuc rac dricwe⁄
ithred . imattrec guẏdi darffo .
Nẏdichuenic but pedi . ẏſguell
delli urth auo . ac imganlin a⁄
deduit . a dioffrid aaduo . aw⁄
na mẏnich enuuẏret . Ȯrdivet
afeʀlinho .

THE DREAM

I had a dream last night:
cute
would be its interpreter.
One may not relate
its naughtiness:
who has not seen it
will not know.....
  leading a host
  is a fine thing;
  a locality's cowardice
  doesn't make for pride.....
I was under the same coverlet
as a fair maiden
of the hue of the wave
among the pebbles.....
  working for the good
  is no tribulation;
  those who are not worthy
  will have cause to remember;
  worse -
  to proffer an answer
  to those with no notion;
  transgression is not removed
  by remorse
  after its perpetration;
  no benefit accrues
  from worrying;
  it's better to hold on to
  what will be,
  follow the blessed,
  give up earthly pleasures;
  whoever does frequent wrong
  will finally be overtaken.

Moli duu innechrev
a diuet. Ae kẏn⁄
iw nẏ welli nẏ om⁄
et. Vn mab meiʀ modri⁄
daw teeʀnet. meir mam
criſt ergẏnan rianet. Dẏ⁄
dav ẏr heul oʒ duẏrein ir
goglet. Dẏ eiraul ir dẏ.
maur drugaret. Aʀ dẏ
mab iolud en karet. Duv
uchom. Duu ragom. Duu
vet. Ren new anʀotone

ran trugaret . Teẏrn uron.
tanc ẏ romne. heb imomet
Diwẏccomne a digonhom
o gamuet . Kin mẏnedim
gueꞧid imiꞧuet. in tẏwill
heb canvill im goꝛſſet .Ẏm
Gueinvod im goꝛod im goꝛ⁄
wet. guẏdi meiꞧch ac im⁄
tuiɴ glaſſuet. a chẏuet a⁄
chid im agraget . Nẏ chiſ⁄
gaw gobuẏllaw om diw⁄
et. Gulad it im ne . ẏſag⁄

ro ẏ maſſvet . mal deil ovla⁄
en guit daduet . Guae ag⁄
aur agrauɴ maur ueʀth⁄
et . ac onyſguataul ẏ ʀiet.
Kẏn gatteʀ ew in ʀẏred.
preſſen.p̣ẏgil uit inẏ di⁄
vet . Nẏ vir drud . nid
ẏſcrid inẏ timhẏr. Nẏ chi⁄
uid uoze . nẏ chiueirch .
nid eiſtet . nẏ chan wen
nid eirch trugaret . Bit
chuero ẏ talhaur inẏ di⁄

wet . Sẏ beʀuid . a maurw⁄
rid. a maʀet. Meithriɴ co2⁄
ph.ẏ lẏffeint a nadret. a llev⁄
uod ac imtuiɴ enwiret . Ac
agheu dẏdau uʀth gluẏdet .
Ew in luth dẏ chinull dẏchi⁄
uet . Dẏneffa heneint a lled
aʀnad . Dẏ cluft . di trem .
di teint neud adwet . Dẏ
chricha croen diuiffet . ath⁄
una heneint. a lluidet . An
eiʀolve ne mihagel . aʀ ren
new ran trugaret .

PRAISING GOD

Let's praise God
at the beginning
and the end of time.
Whoever seeks him out
He'll not deny,
not refuse.
The son of Mary
queen-bee of kings,
Mary mother of Christ,
famed of maidens.
The sun will shift
from the east to the north:
out of your great mercy
implore your Son
to put an end to our sinning.

God above us,
God before us.
God rules.
May the King of Heaven
give now the portion of mercy.
Regal bosom,
let there be peace between us
without denial.
May we undo what
we have done,
before going to my earth,
my verdant grave,
all dark without a candle
to my tumulus,
my nook,
my cranny,
my resting place.

After horses
and drinking new mead,

feasting,
making love to women,
I don't sleep,
I think -
about my end:
we are in a land
where pleasaunce
is troubled.....
like leaves,
we,
from the tip
of withered trees.

Woe to the miser
who amasses great riches
and doesn't
give to the glory of God.
Even though he's let off
in the bustle of the present,
in danger he will be
in the end.
The foolhardy doesn't know,
he doesn't tremble
in his time.
He doesn't get up early,
he doesn't greet you,
he doesn't stay put,
he doesn't chant a prayer,
doesn't beg for mercy.
He pays bitterly in the end
for his pride
and pomp
and sway.....
    nurtured the body
    for toads
    and snakes
    and monsters,
    evil done.

And death
will come to the door,
greedily collect,
take away.
Upon you
descend
old age
senility;
hearing
sight
bite
fade
away.....
the skin of your fingers
shrivels,
this
has ageing
greying
wrought.

    May Saint Michael beg for us
    mercy's portion
    from the King of Heaven.

Kinte´
viɴ keinhaw amſſer. Dẏar
adaʀ glas callet . Ereidiʀ
in ʀich . ich iguet . Guirt
moƶ brithottoƶ tiret . Ban
ganhont cogev aʀ blaen
guit guiw handid muẏ.
vẏ llauuridet . Toſt muc
amluc anhunet . kan eth´
int uẏ keʀeint in attwet .
ẏm bʀin in tẏno.ininẏſſet
moƶ impop foƶt itelheʀ.rac

crift guiɴ nid oes inialet.
Oet in chuant in car ītro´
ffet treitau tẏ tir dẏalltu´
det . Seith feint afeith´
ugeint . afeithcant . aw´
ant in un o2ffet . ẏ gid a
crift guiɴ .nẏ fo2thint ve
vẏgilet . Rec aarchawe
nim naccer . ẏ rof a duv .
dagnouet . Ambo fo2th .
ẏ po2th riet . Crift nẏbu´
ve trift ẏtho2ffet .

MAYTIME THOUGHTS

Maytime is the nicest time,
birds are loud,
trees are green;
ploughs are in the furrow,
oxen in the yoke.
The sea is green,
lands have many colours.

When cuckoos sing
on the tops of fine trees,
sadness
grows.

Smoke stings,
at night I'm all too restless
since my loved ones
have gone to the grave.

On hill,
in hollow,
on islands in the sea,
everywhere you go
before blessed Christ
there is no place that is God-forsaken.

In desire,
in lust,
in transgression,
it is time
to make for
the land of your final retreat.
Seven saints,
seven score,
seven hundred
gone in one convocation:
with Christ the blessed

dread ·
they do not suffer.

A boon I ask,
may you not refuse me:
let there be peace
between God and me.
Let there be for me
a way to the gate of glory.
Amongst your people
Christ
I mayn't be sad.

Gogonedauc argluit
hanpich guell. Athuē⁄
dicco de egluiſ. achagell. A.
kagell . ac egluis . A. vaſt⁄
ad . a diffuis . A . Teir fin⁄
haun ẏ ſſit . Due uch guīt.
ac vn uch eluit . A . ẏrif⁄
gaud aʀ dit . A . Siʀic aᵱ⁄
wit . Athuendiguiſte aw⁄
raham pen fit . A . vuchet
tragiuit . A. aᵭaʀ aguen⁄
en . A. attᵱauʀ. a dieɴ.

Athuendigufte aron amo⟨
efen. A ⸱vafcul a femen. A.
Seithnieu a seʀ. A . awiʀ.
ac etheʀ. A . llevreu a llẏ⟨
theʀ. A . pifcaud in hẏdiʀ⟨
ueʀ. A . kẏwid . a gueith⟨
red . A . tẏuvod a thẏdued.
A . ẏ faul da digoned. Ath⟨
uendigaf de argluit gogo⟨
ned . Gogonedauc . a. h.ɢ.

BLESSED BE THE LORD

Glorious God,
all hail.
May church and chancel
bless you,
may lowland and highland
bless you,
may the three fountains
bless you,
two above the wind,
one above the earth;
may darkness and daylight
bless you,
may satin and fruit-trees
bless you.

Abraham blessed you,
the father of the faith:
life eternal blessed you,
birds and bees blessed you,
blessed you
stubble and grass.

Moses and Aeron blessed you,
male and female blessed you,
seven days and stars blessed you,
air and atmosphere blessed you,
books and letters blessed you,
fish in the torrent blessed you,
mind and act blessed you,
sand and soil blessed you,
blessed you
all the good that's done.

I bless you,
Lord of Majesty,
Glorious God,
all hail.

Rᵈuireaue. tri trined in
celi.ẏſſi un a thri.vn´
ed un ẏnni. vnguiꞰth oe
teithi. un duu diuoli. ath´
uolaſ uaurri maur dẏ uꞰ´
hidꞰi. Dẏuolaur. ẏſguir.
Dẏuolaudir ẏſ mi. ẏſbud
baꞰtoni aꞰhelv eloẏ. Han´
pich guell criſti. pater. &.
ſili. & ſp̄u. domni. on. ad´
onaẏ. AꞰduireaue Dev.
ẏſſi vn a Deu. ẏſſi tri hep
ev. hep haut ẏamhev. Aw´
naeth fruith afreu a fop.

amriffreu.Duu ẏenv.in Deu.
Duẏuaụ ẏ kẏffreu.Duu ẏenv.
in tri Duẏuuaul ẏ inni.Duu
ẏenu invn.Duu paulac an´
nhuN. Ᾱrduẏreaue. vn. iſ´
ẏ Deu ac uN. iſſi tri aR nuN.iſ´
ſi Duu ẏ huN. aunaeth maur´
th a lluN.amaſcul abuN.ac
nat kẏuoʒuN baſ ac anot´
uN.Auneth tuim ac oeR. a.
heul alloeR.a llẏthir .ig.
Cuir a fflam im pabuir.a.
ſerch in ſinhuir. abuN hẏg´
aR huiR.alloſci.pimp kaeR
otẏueti.wiR . ❧❧❧❧❧❧❧❧❧❧❧❧

TO THE TRINITY

Trinity in heaven,
I extol you.
One in Three,
one unit of energy.
In divine right
one miracle,
one God to be praised.

Great King
I praise you,
great is your manhood.
Praise to you is true,
I am your extoller.
To be laureate
at Eloi's behest
is indeed benefit.
Greetings, Christ,
father and son
and the spirit of God.

I extol God
who is one and two,
who is three -
no lie,
and doubting him
no walkover -
he who made fruit and flow
and the world's miscellany:
God whose name is two,
whose word is divine,
God whose name is three,
whose energy is divine;
God whose name is one,
the God of Paul and Anthony.

One I extol
who is two and one,
who is three together,
who is God himself;
the one who made
Tuesdays and Mondays
man and woman
that shallows and depths
are not one;
who made hot and cold,
sun and moon,
a letter in wax
flame in a wick
love in sensibility,
and a maiden,
beloved, gentle:
did the sacking of five castles
for their fornication.

Win ẏ bid hi ẏ vedwen in diffrin guẏ. Afirth
ẏchegev pop vn. pop dvẏ. Ac auit pan vo. ẏ
gad in ardudvẏ. A chimrevan biv am rid vochn͗
vẏ. A᾿pheleidir a gaur inẏganhvẏ. Ac edwin imoɴ.
ban gluedichuẏ. Ar gueiſſon gleiſſon ẏſcawin t̃͗
vodi. ar dillad rution in ev roti ⬤⬤⬤⬤⬤⬤⬤⬤⟶

Win ẏ bid hi ẏ vedwen. ẏmpimlumon. a
Wil ban vit ban baran eilon. Ac awil. ẏ.
freigc in lluricogion. ac am gewin ir aeluid bv͗
id balawon᾿a mineich in vẏnich in varchogioɴ.

Win ẏbid hi ẏ veduen ẏguarthaw din͗
vẏthuẏ. A vibid ban vo ẏgad in ardud͗
wẏ: Ar peleidir kẏchuin amedrẏwuẏ . A .
phont ar taw. ac arall ar tawuẏ. Ac arall
amwall am dwẏlan gwy. Ar saer ae gunel͗
wẏ. bid ẏ env garvẏ. Arbenẏgaul mon ae.
guledẏchuẏ. Guraget dan ẏgint. Guir ẏg kẏſtvẏ.
Dedwẏtach no mi ae harhowe. Amſer kadwal͗
adiʀ. keʀt a ganhwi. ⬤⬤⬤⬤⬤⬤⬤⬤⬤⬤⬤⬤

BIRCHES

Blessed is the birch tree
in the valley of the Wye,
its branches falling
now one at a time,
now two,
and will be there
when the battle rages in Ardudwy,
the lowing of cattle
around the ford of Mochnwy,
spears and battle-cry in Degannwy,
and Edwin in Anglesey
when he takes over,
the young greenhorns
fighting diffidently,
being decked out
in blooded garments.

Blessed is the birch tree in Pumlumon
which will watch
when people's fury will be high
and will see the French
decked out in armour
and in the back of the hearth
food for monsters -
and monks
often
will be horsemen.

Blessed is the birch tree
on the top of Dinfythwy
which will know
when the battle rages in Ardudwy
the dart of the phalanx
for Edryfwy,
the crossing of the Taf,
the other over Tawe,

yet another destruction
on the two banks of the Wye;
and the wringer of this havoc
his name will Garwy be,
the topmost man in Anglesey
will govern them
with women
windswept
and men
beaten up.

A happier one than me
awaits it,
the time of Cadwaladr,
a poem
will he sing to it.

fallen ꝑen ꝑ ẏ chageu. puwaur maur weri
rauc enwauc in vev. Ami diſgoganave rac
ꝑchen machrev. Jn diffrin machavuẏ mer⸗
chẏrdit crev. goʒuolet ẏ loegẏr goʒgoch
lawnev. Oian aparchellan dẏdau dẏwiev. goʒ⸗
volet ẏgimrẏ goʒuaur gadev. Jn amuiɴ kẏmi⸗
naud clefẏtaud clev. Aer o ſaeſſon. ar onn verev.
A guarwẏaur pelre ac ev pennev. Ami dẏſgogana
fe gwir heb gev. Dẏrchaſaud maban inadvan
ẏ dehev. A fallen ꝑen pren hẏduf glas. Pv
waur ẏ chagev hẏ ae chein wanaſ. Ami dẏſ⸗
goganafe kad amdias. Penguern kẏwetẏrn.
met ẏ hataſ. ⧲⧲⧲⧲⧲⧲⧲⧲⧲⧲⧲⧲⧲⧲⧲⧲⧲⧲⧲⧲⧲⧲⧲
[ac am gẏlch kẏminawd kẏmẏn leaſ eingẏl.
gan pendeuic erẏri eri attkaſ.]

Awallen pen . A pren melin . a.ᐟ
tȳw in hal art . heb art inẏchilchᐟ
in . A mi difcoganwe kad impʀẏdin . Jn amᐟ
vin ev terwin aguir duliɴ . Seithlog.ẏdeuant
drof lẏdan liɴ . A Seith cant . drof moʒ ẏ oʒefkiɴ.
Orfaul ẏdeuant . nẏdant ẏ kenhin . Namuiɴ.
Seith lledwac gwẏdi ev llettkinͳ⸺ ∽∽∽∽∽∽

Wallen pen . Atẏf tra ʀuɴ . Kẏmaethliffᐟ
vne inẏbon . irbot ẏ wuɴ . Amẏfcud.
arwẏ ifguit . Am clet ar wẏ clun . Ac ẏg coed.
Keliton ẏ kifceiffe vẏ hun . Oian apchellan.
pir puẏllutte huɴ . Andaude adar clẏwir
ev hẏmevtuɴ . Teernet drof moʒ adav dẏv.
llun . Guin ev bid ve kẏmri oʒ arowuɴ.

Wallen pen atif inllanerch . ẏhangeᐟ
rt ae hargel rac riev ʀẏderch . amfaᐟ
thir inẏbon . maon ẏnẏchilch . Oet aelav vt

vt dulloet diheueirch. Nu nẏm cari guendit
ac nimeneirch. Oef kaſ gan gwaſſauc guaeſſ′
af Rẏdirch. Rẏrewineiſ ẏ mab aemerch. ag′
hev aduc paup. pa rac nam kẏueirch. a.
guẏdi guendolev nep riev impeirch. Nẏm gogauɴ
guarvẏ. nẏm goffvẏ goʒterch. ac igueith arẏw
derit. oet eur. wẏ goʒthoʒch. Kin buẏf. aelav
hetiv gan eiliv eleirch. ⚭⚭⚭⚭⚭⚭⚭⚭⚭⚭⚭⚭⚭⚭

Afallen pen. blodev eſſplit. atiff inargel in
argoẏdit. Chuetlev agiklev ir inechrev
dit. Rẏſſoʒri guaſſauc guaeſſaf. meuſit
Duẏweith atheiʀgueith. pedeirgueith in vn.
dit. Och ieſſu. nadẏffv wẏnihenit. kẏn dẏf′
fod ar willave lleith mab guendit. ⚭⚭⚭⚭⚭⚭⚭

Afallen pen atiff ar lan. afon. Jnẏ llurv.
nẏ lluit maer. i̯nẏchlaer aeron. Trafu
vm puẏll. waſtad. am buiad inibon. a.
Bun wen wariuſ. vn weinuſ vanon. Dec mli′
net adev ugein inẏgein anetwon. it viſ inẏm′
teith gan willeith agwillon. Guẏdi da di′
ogan aditan kertoʒion. Nv nev nam guẏ.
guall. gan wẏlleith aguẏllon. Nv nev nach′
ẏſcafe ergrinaf. wẏnragon. Vẏ argluit guen′
dolev am broʒrẏv brodoʒion. Guẏdi poʒthi heint
ahoed amcẏlch coed Keliton. Buẏf guaſ guinwẏ′
dic. gan guledic goʒchoʒtion. ⚭⚭⚭⚭⚭⚭⚭⚭⚭⚭⚭⚭

Afallen pen blodev effplit. a tẏf igwerid ag͗
hűd ẏguit. Difgogan hwimleian hwet͗
il adiwit. id lathennaur gan brid gur͗
hid erwit. Rac dreigev arderchev. riev Rẏbit. Go2͗
uit grat wehin din digrefit. Rac maban hvan
heolit arweit. Saeffon ardiwreit beirt ar kin͗
Afallen pen apren fion attif ẏ dan ⌐ .it.
gel ẏg coed Keliton. Kid keiffeer ofer vit
heruitẏhaton. inẏdel kadwaladir oe kinadil .
kadwaon. ẏ erir tẏwi ateiwi affon. adẏuod.
grande o aranwinion. a guneuthur guar. o.
willt. o gwallt hiꝛion. ∞∞∞∞∞∞∞∞∞∞∞∞∞

Afallen pen apren fion. attif. ẏdan gel ẏg
coed Keliton. Kid keiffer ofer vit he͗
rwit. ẏ hafon. ẏnẏ del kadwaladir oe kin͗
adẏl. ꝛid Reon. Kinan inẏerbin ef kẏchw͗
in ar faeffon. Kimrẏ ao2vit kein bid eudra͗
gon. Kaffaud paub ẏ teithi. llauen vi bri. brẏ͗
thon. Kenhitto2 kirrn eluch. kathil hetuch

⌐ a hinoɴ.

70

MERLIN'S APPLE-TREES

Sweet apple-tree
with branches sweet,
fruit-bearing
much valued
famed
my very own,
before the owner of Machrau
I prophesy
in the valley of Machafwy
on bloody Wednesday
triumph for the English
with their all too red blades.
Ah, little piglet,
come Thursday
there'll be triumph
for the Welsh
in enormous struggles
warding off the thrust,
the swift strike
with spears of ash
giving the English
a hammering,
playing football
with their heads.
I prophesy the truth
without falsehood:
a young lad will arise
in the territory of the South.

Sweet apple-tree
luxuriant
green,
with laiden branches
and fine base
I prophesy

a dire battle;
the revellers of Pengwern,
mead will be their recompense,
and all around the reaper
English to the sickle put
by the venonous bile
of the lord of Eryri.

Sweet apple-tree
you golden bough
that grows on the edge
I prophesy a battle in Pictland
defending their boundary
with the men of Dublin.
In seven ships they'll come
over a wide lake
and seven hundred strong
over sea to overcome us:
of those who get here,
with us they will not come
except seven
empty heads
gone empty-handed.

Sweet apple-tree
that grows beyond the Rhun...
at its base
I had fought
for a maiden's bliss
with shield on shoulder
and sword on hip,
and I myself slept
in the forest of Celyddon.
O little piglet,
why are you thinking of sleep?
Listen to the birds' pleading.
Kings
will come Monday

over the sea.
Blessed be the Welsh
from their conspiring.

Sweet apple-tree
that in Llanerch grows,
its mystique
will hide it
from Rhydderch the king.
Bustle at its foot,
lands all around it,
they had treasure,
brave cohorts:
now Gwenddydd doesn't love me,
doesn't greet me.
I am hated by Gwasawg,
Rhydderch's protector:
I brought about the ruin
of his son and daughter.
Death took everybody away,
that is why they don't talk to me.
Now that Gwenddolau's gone,
no king respects me.
Teasing is no pleasure,
no woman comes to look me up.
And in the battle of Arfderydd
I wore a golden torque:
today I've become the plaything
of a couple of swans.

Sweet apple-tree
with splendid flowers,
that grows in a nook in Argoedydd.
Tales did I hear tell
at the beginning of the day,
that Gwasawg the defender of riches
fulminates against me,
not twice

but three times,
four times
in one day.
O Jesus,
would that my end had come,
before coming on my hand
the blood of the son
of Gwenddydd.

Sweet apple-tree
that grows on the river bank -
because of the current
no steward can make it
to its glistening fruit -
when I was in my right mind
I was to be found at its foot
with a fair, playful maid,
a slender lemmun.
Ten years and two score
have I been
moving along
through twenty bouts of madness
with wild ones in the wild;
after not so dusty things
and entertaining minstrels,
only lack does now keep me company
with wild ones
in the wild.
I don't sleep now,
I tremble,
my dragon,
my lord Gwenddolau
and my nearest and dearest.
After suffering illness
and longing
around the forest of Celyddon,
let me be
a blissful hireling

with the Lord of Hosts.

Sweet apple-tree
with splendid flowers
that grows
in grounds
with an assortment of trees,
Chwyfleian prophesies,
she tells a tale:
spears will be cast
with the intent
born of keen courage
before exalted dragon kings.
A leap of destruction
will down
a man with no religion.
Before a youth like the sun
with daring ways
will the English
be uprooted
and bards flourish.

Sweet apple-tree
with flowers foxglove pink
that grows in secret
in the forest of Celyddon,
and even though
you look for it
it is all in vain
because of its peculiarity
until Cadwaladr comes
from his meeting of warriors
to the lowland of Tywi
and the river Teifi
with the terrible horde
of palefaces -
to tame the wild
with the long hair.

Sweet apple-tree
with flowers foxglove pink
that grows in secret
in the forest of Celyddon,
and even though
you look for it
it is all in vain
because of its peculiarity
until Cadwaladr comes
from his meeting of warriors
in Rhyd Reon -
Cynan in response
setting out for the English.
The Welsh will win,
glorious shall their dragon be:
everybody shall have their rights,
the Brythons' morale will be high,
the horns of celebration
will be blown,
the song
of peace,
of prosperity.

O Jan aparchellan . A parchell dedwit . Nachlat
dẏredcir ẏmpen minit . Clat in lle argel in arcoe⁄
dit. Rac erwiſ ritech hael ruẏfadur fit. A mi diſcogan⁄
aſe a gwir uit . Hid in aber taradir rac trauſev prẏ⁄
dein kimrẏ oll inẏeu kẏfluit . llẏuelin ẏ env o ei ſſillit
gwinet gur digoᴢbit . ∞∞∞∞∞∞∞∞∞∞∞∞∞∞

O Jan aparchellan . Oet reid myned rac .
Kinẏtion moᴢdei bei llafaſſed . Rac diuod
erlid arnamne ac in gueled . ᴀc oᴢ diaghune .
nẏ chuinune in lluted . ᴀmi diſgoganaſe . rac
ton naᵛed . Rac vnic bariffviᴎ gvehin dived .
dirchaſaud llogaud nid ir llettcred ẏn tẏ⁄
mhir gurthtir a guẏſtuiled . in ẏ del kin⁄
an iti oechin gueled . nẏ bit attcoᴢ bith ar

O Jan aparchellan ⌠. ẏthrefred . ∞∞∞
Nẏhaut kiſſcaf. rac godurt ẏ gal⁄
ar ẏ ſſit arnaf . Deg mlinet a deu ugein
ẏd poᴢtheiſe poen ẏſtruc a oᴢhoen ẏ ſſit
arnaf . Oes imi gan ieſſv gaffv guaeſſaf
brenhinoet newoet achoet uchaf . Nẏm⁄
ad rianed o plant adaw . ar nẏ creddoe

77

ẏ dovit in dit diwethaf . Ẏd welefe guen⁄
dolev in perthic riev . in cẏnull preitev opop
eithaw . ẏ dan vẏguerid ʀut nv neud araf.
pen teernet gogėet llaret mvẏhaw .

Jan aparchellan oet reid gweti .
Rac offin pimp penaeth o noₐtman⁄
di . Ar pimhed in mẏned drof moₐ
heli . ẏ oₐefkin iwerton tirion trewi . Ef guna⁄
haud rẏuel a dififfci . ac arfev coch . ac och in⁄
di . Ac winttuẏ in dihev a doant o heni . ac.
awnant enʀẏdet ar bet . Dewi . Ami difgo⁄
ganafe bid divifci . o ẏmlat mab a thad gu⁄
lad ae guẏbi . a mẏned ẏ loegruif diffuif tre⁄
wi . Ac na bo guared bith ẏ noₐtmandi .
Jan aparchellan . Na uit hunauc .
Rẏ dibit attamne chuetil dẏfrida⁄
uc . penaetheu bẏchein anudonauc . Meiri
mangaled am pen keinhauc . Pan diffon .
drof moₐ guir eneichauc . Kad meirch . ẏ⁄
danunt ve . dev wẏnepauc . Deuwlaen . ar⁄

euguaev anoleithauc . ᴇʀti heb medi ẏmbid
dẏhetauc . guell bet . no buhet pop ẏghenauc .
Cirrn ar ẏ guraget pedrẏfanhauc . A ffan⸗
vont ve coᵹfoᵹion meibon eidauc . ẏ bit bo⸗
re taer . rac Kaer fallauc . ⊜⊜⊜⊜⊜⊜⊜⊜⊜⊜⊜⊜

O Jan aparchellan . aparchell dẏhet
Rimdẏuueid huimleian chuetẏl enrẏ⸗
uet . ami difcoganaue haf guithlonet . kẏw⸗
 rug brodoᵹion brad owinet . Ban diholeʀ ta⸗
guiftil inhiʀ otir guinet . Dẏbit feith ganll̊g
oẏnt gan wint goglet ac inabeʀ clev eukin⸗

O Jan aparchellan aparchell Ꞁ. atlet .
guin . Rẏmdẏwọd huimleian chuetil
amechrin . Pan bebillo lloegir in tir ethlin . a.
guneuthur dẏganhuẏ dinaf degin . o g✳✳✳✳✳✳✳
lloegir allẏuelin aduit mab aʀwarr . a✳✳✳✳✳

kẏchuin . Ban foꝛro deinoel mab dunaud

deinwin . ad vit frangc ar ffo foꝛt nẏ ofin . Jn

aber dulaſ . gvanaſ guehin . Cochuet in ev

kẏlwet . ẏn ev kilchiɴ . ᙇᙇᙇᙇᙇᙇᙇᙇᙇᙇᙇᙇᙇᙇᙇᙇᙇᙇᙇᙇᙇ

Oian aparchellan hoian hoiev . Bei ẏche⁓
nauc duv gunai . ẏmchuelev . Y parche⁓
ll ẏ ſſẏ.wiv . bitaud mev . ar hun ẏ ſſẏ ✶✶✶✶
keiſſed in tev . ᙇᙇᙇᙇᙇᙇᙇᙇᙇᙇᙇᙇᙇᙇᙇᙇᙇᙇᙇᙇᙇ

Oian aparchellan neud dit golev . An⁓
daude leiſ adar duffẏʀ dẏar leiſſev .
an bit ni bluitinet a hiʀ diev . areiv enwir.

edwi fʀuẏtheu . ac eſcib . lluch lladron diffeith

llannev . amẏneich aoʙʀin beich obechodev .

Oian aparchellan llim ẏ vinet . Kẏuuelẏ
anwinud panelhute ẏ oꝛuet . Bẏchan
a wir rẏderch hael heno ẏ ar ẏ wlet . a poꝛth⁓

eiſe neithuir o anhunet . Eiri hid impen

clun. gan cuɴ callet . Pibonvẏ imblev. blin

wẏ Rẏſſet . Rẏ dibit div mauꝛͭͪ dit guith⸗

lonet . Kẏwrug glẏu powis achlaſ guinet.

Achivod hirell oe hir oʒwet . ẏ ꝺmviɴ ae el⸗

iṇ terwin guinet . Ac onẏmbit gan vẏ Rii

ran trugaret . Guae wi ban imbv. trv vẏ

Oian aparchan . Nẏ bit ⌐diwet .

kẏwun . Ban kẏhuin llu aer oka⸗

er wẏRtin . Ẏ harduẏ dev kenev. in kẏwre⸗

nhin . o hil Riſ aerllut . aer llẏſ bitin . Ban

llather ẏ ſaeſſon ẏ kimerev trin . Guin ev.

bid vẏ kimri . kimrvẏ . werin . ⊗⊗⊗⊗⊗⊗⊗⊗

Oian aparchellan. aparchell . guiɴ gviſ .

Nachuſte hun boʒe . nachlat impriſc .

Rac dẏuod . Riderch hael . ꝺe cvn kẏſruẏs .

Kin caffael ohonautte ẏ coed reddaud. dẏchuis.

※ Nẏchirchud diffeith odiffuis liN.

Oian aparchellan aparchell guin. Bei
guelud a weleis o treis degin. Nẏchẏ/
ſcute hun bere . nẏchclatude brin.※ Ban eiſte/
tho ſaeſſon inẏſarffren . achirchu opell caſtell
gollwin atuit dillad hoev agloev dullin.

※ Ban diſſon noʒtmin . ẏ ar llidan llin ad vit imurthrin ina gan vitinaur . a goʒeſcin pdein ẏ uiron ẏſwein ar vall o lundein adẏattavr. a mi

Oian aparchellan andaude ẏnaur ban
dottint .ve. guir guinet ev gueith ma/
ur . llaffnev in ertirn kirn aganhaur . Briuha/
ud llurugev rac llim waewaur . A※mi diſgoga/
naue . Deu podaur . a luniont tegnevet oneſ.
hid laur . Kẏnan kadwaladir . Kẏmri penbal/
adir . bitaud ev kinatil aedmẏccaur . A chiurei/
thau gulad. achiſtutia gwad . allv alledrad a
divahaur . An bi ni inaeth guared guẏdi gu/
aeth . Neb ohaelonaeth nididolaur.

Oan aparchellan. Nud glas minit ten⁄
ev vẏ llen imi nẏd llonit. lluid ẏv. vẏ
bleit nim treit guendit. Ban diffont guir.
brineirch irguaʀth luit. Kimri aoʒuit kein
bid ev dit.◦◦◦◦◦◦◦◦◦◦◦◦◦◦◦◦◦◦◦◦◦◦◦

Oan aparchellan. aparchell gawi. Na
chlat de redkir nac iſte.wiuuẏ. Nac a⁄
char waes. Nachar.warvẏ. Achuſſil arotafe
ẏ wenabuẏ. Nauid ieuangc ſerchauc ſẏberv
warruẏ. Ami diſcoganafe gueith machav⁄
vi. Aduit geloʒaur ʀut in ʀiv didmuẏ. O ki⁄
wranc ẏ kẏnvrein bron renion kifrvi. Advit
boʒe och. ac och ofuẏ. Arth odeheubarth adir⁄
chafuẏ. Rẏllettaud ẏwir ew tra thir mẏnvẏ
Guini bid hi guendit aeharovẏ ban.vo pende⁄
wic dẏued aeguledichuẏ. ◦◦◦◦◦◦◦◦◦◦◦◦◦

OJan aparchellan neud blodeu drein goꝛlaſ kei⁄
n minit eluit neud kin. Ami diſcoganaue.
kad coed lluiueiɴ.ageloꝛaur rution rac ruthir
Owein. Ban gunelhont meiriev datlev bichein. An⁄
udon abrad gulad veibonin. Aphan del kadualadir
ẏ oꝛeſcin mon dileaur ſaeſon otirion pʀẏdein. ⊏====⊐

OJan aparchellan maur eriſſi auit impͥdein ac
nim doꝛbi. Ban diffon brodoꝛion oamtiret.
mon.ẏ holi brithon brithuid dẏbi. Dirchaſ⁄
aud dreic ſaud ſau iſpi gurt kẏuan uaran o lan.
teiwi. Gunahaud am dẏued digiuẏſci. Bit itau
in aelau eilon indi. ⊗⊗⊗⊗⊗⊗⊗⊗⊗⊗⊗⊗⊗⊗⊗⊗⊗⊗

OJan apchellan. Moꝛ enʀẏuet na bit un enhid
ẏ bid inunwet. Pelled ſon ſaeſſon ſeil kẏuriſſ;
arbrithon haelon hil kẏmuẏet. Ami diſco⁄
ganaue kindiguet. Brithon dros ſaeſſon bʀithuir
aemet. Ac ina indaune daun goꝛuolet. Guidi bod
inhiʀ inhuir.vʀidet. ⊗⊗⊗⊗⊗⊗⊗⊗⊗⊗⊗⊗⊗⊗⊗⊗⊗⊗

OJan apchellan andaude ireilon agroar ad⁄
ar kir kaerreon. Vnẏſſun aroun minit ma⁄
on ẏ edrich drichinnauc drich ſerchogion.

Ami difcoganawe. Kad ar ẏton. A chad machav⁄
vẏ. Achad avon. Achad coᷦmochno. Achad immon.
Achad kẏminaud. Achad caerlleon. Achad aber gwe⁄
ith. Achad ieithion. Aphan vo diwed tir ᴛeʀwin. ẏ.
eiloɴ. Maban dirchavaud mad. ẏ Vʀẏthoɴ. ⊗⊗⊗⊗⊗⊗
Ꜧoian aparchellan. Bẏdan avit. Moᷦtruan. ẏ.
dẏuod ɑc ew dẏbit. Moᷦẏnion moelon. guraget
revit. Karant nẏpharchant eu kerenhit. Rvit nẏ
kẏwruit. vrth ẏgilit. Efcẏp agkẏueith diffeith difid.
Ꜧoian aparchellan bichan brẏchni. Andaude
leis adar. mẏr. maur ev hinni. Kertoᷦion all⁄
an heb ran teithi. Kẏn fafont inẏdrvs tluf nẏf
deupi. Rẏmdivod gwẏllan opell ẏmi. Tᶒerɳet en⁄
rẏuet ev kiniweti. Gwitil abrithon aromani. ɑv⁄
vnahont dẏhet adivẏfci. Ac ẏ kẏwenv dẏwiev
divod iti. Ac imlat intaer am dvẏlan tẏwi.

Hoian aparchellan. Býchan breichvraſ. Andav
de leis adar moʒ maur eu diaſ. Kertoʒion allan
heb ran vrdaſ. Gurthwnaud eſpid a brid gan gwas.
Heb cadvid. výnep heb ran vʀdaſ. Ban. vo. dev bro׳
der. Deu itaſ am tir. Megittoʒ oc ev guir. vý. hir alaná.

Hoian aparchellan. Ným dawe kingid. Oclýb׳
od lleis adar duwir dýar ev grid. Tenev gvallt
vý pen. Vý llen nýd clid. Dolit vý iſcubaur. nýd ma׳
ur. vý id. Vý crauɴ haw ami nid im verid. Kýn iſ׳
car aduv ditaul kývid. Ami diſcoganawe kiɴ.
goʒffen bid. Gwraget heb gvilet. Gwir heb gurhid.

Hoian aparchellan aparchell rými. Tenev
vý llen nid llonit ými. Ýr gueith arýwderit
mi nýmdoʒbi kýnduguitei awir ý lavʀ. allýr.
enlli. Ami dýſgoganawe góýdi henri. breenhin
na breenhin brithwýd dýbi. ban vo pont. ar.

taw. Ac arall ar týwi. ýdav ý dýved rývel iti

THE OHS OF MYRDDIN

Oh little piglet,
oh happy porker,
don't dig about in your sty
on the top of the mountain,
forage in the hidden place
in Argoedydd
away from the fierce
Rhydderch the Generous,
the tiller-man of the faith...
I prophesy
and it is the truth:
right up to the mouth of Taradr
before the nasties of Britain
all the Welsh will be lined out;
Llywelyn
whose name is from the line
of Gwynedd
is the man
who will carry the day.

Oh little piglet,
we had to go
away from the hunters of the halls
and all the daring-do,
lest revenge come upon us
lest we're found out.
And if we escape
we'll not moan in our ranks,
I prophesy
the coming of the ninth wave
the one and only snow-beard
in the doing of Dyfed.
A monastery will rear its head,
not for the backsliders
in the terrain
of mountains and monsters.

Until Cynan comes back
to defend her,
to her dwellings
there will be no return.

Oh little piglet,
I don't sleep easily
for the clangour of grief
that afflicts me.
For two score years and ten
have I suffered anguish,
I'm pining away.
Can Jesus
procure for me
the protection
of the kings in heaven
with the best lineage.
Of Adam's children;
under a bad sign born
is the one
who does not believe in the Lord
on the last day.
I saw Gwenddolau
a powerful king
gathering booty
far and wide.
Under my red earth
is he now
all quiet like,
the greatest
king of the North,
the greatest too
in tenderness.

Oh little piglet,
we needed prayer
for fear of five premiers
from Normandy,

number five
going over the salty sea
to take over Ireland
of the gentle towns.
He will make war and commotion,
weapons cochineal,
expletive woe.
And they surely will come over
to honour the grave of Dewi.
And I prophesy commotion:
the land will know
of sons turned agaist their fathers;
the English will see
their towns laid waste,
and to the Normans be no quarter given.

Oh little piglet,
don't doze off.
A tragic tale
will reach our ears,
of paltry chiefs
who do not keep their word.
Stingy little stewards
poring over a penny,
when speedy men
will come over the sea
two-faced
with war-horses under them,
two heads
to their inexorable spears.
Of plots with no harvesting
in an unquiet world,
better then to be dead
than to be poor and needy;
women with peaks
on their four-cornered hats
and when men full of lust
will be on the job

a morning of reckoning
it will be
on Salisbury Plain.

Oh little piglet,
oh restless grunter,
Chwyfleian tells me
a wondrous tale:
and I prophesy
a summer of discontent:
from Gwynedd
treachery between brothers
when peace will long
be banished
from the land of Gwynedd.
And seven hundred ships
will wend their way
with the Northern wind
and their meet
will be Milford Haven.

Oh little piglet,
oh blissful pig,
Chwyfleian told
a tale that makes me shake:
when England tents down
in the land of Eddlyn
and Degannwy made
a castle to stand firm
in the clash between
the English and Llywelyn,
a youth will dive
and dart:
when Deiniol the son of Dunawd Deinwyn
loses his cool
the French will run
no matter where.
In Aber Dulas will be

the pillar of destruction,
wreaking carnage,
pallid terror
all around.

Oh little piglet,
oh of ohs,
in dire straits,
for God would cause setbacks,
is any bacon saved:
let that lot be mine -
let *her*
go for the sleep
of death.

Oh little piglet,
see the light of day,
listen to the call of the water-fowl,
shrill cries,
years
stretch out
before us,
long
days;
and evil kings
like rotting fruit:
and bishops harbouring
no-good raiders of churches;
monks fully deserving
their burden of sin.

Oh little piglet,
with your sharp nails,
discourteous bed-fellow
going to lie down like that.
Rhydderch the Generous
at his carousal
little does he know tonight

the extent
last night
of my insomnia.
Snow to my thighs
surrounded by dingoes,
icicles in my hair,
my glory gone.
Tuesday will see
a day of violence
between the lord of Powys
and the Gwynedd lads;
Hirell will arise
from his long repose
to ward off the enemy
from the frontiers of Gwynedd.
And unless my King
grants me my portion of mercy,
pity me
that my end
was so lamentable.

Oh little piglet,
don't be coy.
When a force sets out
from Carmarthen
led by two whelps,
kings together,
of the line of Rhys
the battle-buffer -
battle-sawing troop,
when the English are slaughtered
in the fight
at Cymerau,
great will be my Welshmen's glee,
steadfast crew.

Oh little piglet,
oh blissful sow,

don't take your morning nap,
don't rummage in the undergrowth,
lest Rhydderch the Generous comes
with his clever hounds,
before you're able to snuffle the roots
that you sweated to find.
Oh little piglet,
oh blissful dam
if you saw
the sheer violence
that I saw,
you wouldn't sleep in the morning,
you wouldn't dig the hillside,
you wouldn't make for the wild
by a desolate lake.
When the English encamp
in Sarffryn
and make from afar
for Collwyn castle,
there will be grand uniforms
and ranks all a-glow.

Oh little piglet,
listen to me now,
when the men of Gwynedd
come and do the really big one,
blades flicked around,
horns blaring,
breastplates will be dented
by sharp spears.
When the Normans come
over the Channel
there will be a clash then
between armies
and Britain taken over
by Owain's band
and the pestilence
will be driven away

93

from London town.
And I foretell
the coming of two claimants,
who
peace
will
make
Cynan and Cadwaladr -
for the whole of Wales
their convocation
will be
the admiration of all.
The laws of the land,
the pain of constriction,
forced oaths
and daylight robbery
will be swept away.
And ours
will be the relief
of fair weather
after foul.
No one will miss out
in the spate of generosity.

Oh little piglet,
hoary is the mountain,
my coverlet is threadbare
my hair is all grey;
Gwenddydd won't find me here,
when the men of Bryneich
come to the mustering of shame,
the Welsh will win,
fine will that day be for them.

Oh little piglet,
oh lively sow,
don't dig around in your sty,
don't eat more than you can take,

don't wish for the open,
less of that desire for play:
for I'll give Gwenabwy some advice,
don't be young and amorous,
playing it hard and fast,
and I foretell the battle of Machafwy;
stretchers
red
there'll
be
in Rhiw Didmwy.
From the combat
of bloated chieftains in the saddle,
will be a morning of woe
and woeful visitation:
a bear from Deheubarth will arise
and his men will spread out
over the lands of Monmouth.
Over the moon
will the waiting Gwenddydd be
when a lord of Dyfed
will be the occupier.

Oh little piglet,
the bramble blossoms sprout,
the ridge of the mountain
is greener than green,
the earth lovely:
and yet I foretell
the battle of Llwyfain woods,
and stretchers
all red
before the rush of Owain:
when dung-bailiffs churn
out chittle-chattle;
the country's paltry men
into perjury and treachery.
And when comes Cadwaladr

to occupy Anglesey,
the English will be wiped out
in the lands of Britain.

Oh little piglet,
in Britain will be
great wonders
that I don't care to know.
When the kinsmen come
from the outer edges of Anglesey
to seek out co-Brythons,
a sorry world will it be,
a dragon will gird up its loins
with famous flight of spears;
anger tough and total
from the banks of the Teifi;
confusion in Dyfed wrought
let the deer therein
be his booty.

Oh little piglet,
it's so strange
that no second is like another.
The sound of the English
is now so far away -
that fundament of strife -
and the Brythons,
magnaminous,
people of affliction...
And I foretell
that before the end
the Brythons
will have the measure of the English,
the old Picts shall rule.
And then
will the endowment
of triumph be given
after being

in our langour
all too long.

Oh little piglet,
listen to the deer,
the birds' twitter
by the castle of Rheon.
I would like to seek out
the mountain of Maon
to look at the stormy
gaze of lovers...
And I foretell
a battle on the banks of Idon,
at Machafwy and at Avon,
a battle at Cors Fochno,
and in Môn,
the battle of Cyminawdd,
of Caerllion,
of Aber Gwaith and Ieithion,
and when for good people
an end will come to the border
a good lad will rise up
for the cause.

Oh little piglet,
there's going to be
a right state of affairs,
so sad is its coming,
but come it will,
girls going bald,
lascivious women,
they shall
love,
not respect their kin.
Getting on with one's fellow
will not be easy.
Inarticulate
no-good bishops

will be running amok.

Oh little piglet,
dappled bundle,
listen to the cry of the sea-birds,
they don't keep still.
Glee-men will be non-grata,
outside,
even though they
stand by the door
they still go a-begging.
A wild man from afar
said to me,
kings will have strange affairs,
the Irish, Brythons and Romans
will cause chaos and unrest.
And on the Thursday foretold
to the valley they'll come
and fierce will be the fighting
on the banks of the Teifi.

Oh little piglet,
strong-legged mite,
listen to the voice of the birds,
so great is their commotion.
Minstrels are rejects,
without their portion of honour,
guests anathema,
we suffer a churl's providence
without saving face,
without our portion of honour.
When two brothers,
two like Idas,
come homing onto the land,
from their truth will be cradled
my long-standing debt
of blood.

Oh little piglet,
I am not filled with designs
when I hear the cry of the water fowl,
their loud commotion.
My hair is going thin,
my covering all threadbare.
My barn is sparse,
my corn is running out.
My summer store,
little good does it do me now,
before bidding farewell to God
of the song everlasting.
I do prophesy
to world's end
women without shame,
men without bravery.

Oh little piglet,
sow in heat,
my covering is threadbare,
I have no peace.
Since the battle of Arfderydd,
it doesn't matter to me
even if the sky falls down
and the oceans flood the earth.
I do prophesy
that after Henry
a king that ain't a king
in a shady world
will come.
When there'll be a bridge on the Taf
and another on the Tywi
war will come to Dyfed.

Betev aegulich ẏ glav . gvir nẏ oʒtẏwna⁄
ſſint vẏ dignav . kerwid . a chivʀid

achav. Betev a̋tut gvitwal . nẏ lleſſeint heb
ẏmtial. gurẏen. moʒien . a moʒial. Betev ae
gvlich kauad. gvẏʀ. nẏ lleſſeint in lledʀad. gwen.
a gurien. a guriad. Bet tedei tad awen . ẏg godir
bʀin aren. ẏnẏdvna ton tolo . Bet dilan llan bev⁄
no. Bet keri cletiſhir. ẏgodir hen egluis . ẏnẏ
diffuis graeande . tarv toʒment. ẏmẏnwent
coʒbre. Bet ſeithenniɴ ſinhuir vann ẏ rug
kaer kenedir a glann. moʒ mauridic a kinran.
En aber gwenoli.̇ ẏ mae bet pʀẏderi. ẏnẏterev
tonnev tir. ẏg karrauc. bet gwallauc hiʀ .
Bet gwalchmei ẏmpẏton. ir diliv.ẏ dẏnetoɴ.
in llan padaʀn bet kinon. Bet gur gwaud
urtin in uchel tẏtiɴ. iniſel gwelitin . bet Kẏn⁄
on mab clẏtno idiɴ ,

Gwẏdi gurum achoch achein . a . goᵤuẏtaur maur minreiᴎ. in llan helet bet.⁓ owein . Gwẏdi gweli agwaedlan . agviſcav ſeir⸜ ch ameirch cann . Neud ew hun bet kintilan.

Eᵢs cul ẏ bet ac ẏſ hir. in llurv llẏauſ am hir. bet meigen ab run ruẏw gwir.

Bet ẏ march . bet ẏ guẏthur . bet ẏ gug⸜ aun cletẏ frut . aᴎoeth bid bet ẏ arthur .

GRAVE POEMS

Those graves
which the rain soaks
are of men
who weren't used
to being baited,
Cerwyd, and Cywryd and Caw.

Those graves
hidden by the bush...
they weren't killed
without being avenged,
Gwrien, Morien and Morial.

Those graves
which the shower wets
are of men
who were not killed
while thieving,
Gwên and Gwrien and Gwriad.

The grave of Tydai
father of the muse
lies in the land of Bryn Aren;
where the wave laps
is the grave of Dylan
in Llanbeuno.

The grave of Ceri Longsword
lies in an old churchyard,
in the stony depths:
in the cemetery of Corbre
lies a battle bull.

The grave of Seithennin
so high-minded,
lies between Caer Cenedr

and a river bank...
such a splendid leader.

In Aber Gwenoli
lies the grave of Pryderi,
where the waves
strike the land.
In Carrawg lies
the grave of Gwallawg
the tall.

The grave of Gwalchmai
lies in Peryddon,
since the flood
of the little people
in Llanbadarn lies
the grave of Cynon.

The grave of a man
of high renown
lies on a lofty height
in low
last repose,
the grave of Cynon
the son of Clydno Eiddin.

After armour,
red feathers,
and finery:
big, tight-lipped
horses
in Llan Heledd
is the grave of Owain.

After wound and blood-let,
the donning of trappings
and white horses
he's all asleep -

here the grave of Cynddylan.

His grave is narrow
it's long,
after a time
with his host
for so long,
the grave of Meigen
the son of Rhun
the leader of many.

There's a grave for March,
one for Gwythyr,
another for Gwgawn Redsword...

The grave of Arthur is a mystery.

Gereint fil' erbin.

Rac gereint gelin kẏstut . ẏ gueleiſe
meirch can crimrut. a gwidẏ gaur garv achlut.
Rac gereint gelin dihad . gueleiſe meirch crimr⁄
ut o kad . a guẏdi gaur garu puẏllad . Rac gereint ge⁄
lin oꝛmes. gueleiſ meirch can eucrees. a guẏdi gaur ga⁄
rv achles. En llogboꝛth ẏgueleiſe vitheint . a geloꝛaur
mvẏ nomeint . a guir rut rac ruthir gereint . Enllo⁄
gboꝛth ẏ gueleiſe giminad. guirigrid aguaed am iad . rac
gereint vaur mab ẏtad . En llogpoꝛth gueleiſe gotto⁄
ev. a guir nẏgilint rac gvaev. ac ẏved gviɴ oguẏdir glo⁄
ev. En llogpoꝛth ẏ gueleiſe arwev guir. a guẏar in din⁄
ev. agvẏdi gaur garv atnev. En llogpoꝛth ẏ gueleiſe . ẏ
arthur guir deur kẏmẏnint a dur . ameraudur llẏw⁄
iaudir llawur. En llogpoꝛth ẏ llaſ ẏ gereint . guir .
deur o odir diwneint . a chin rillethid ve. lla⁄
tẏſſẹnt . Oet re rereint dan voꝛtuid gereīt
garhirion graun guenith . Rution ruthir erir⁄
ion blith. Oet re rerent dan voꝛtuid gereint . garhiriō
graun aebv. Rution ruthir eriron dv. Oet re rereint
dan moꝛtuid gereint . garhirion graun boloch. Rution
ruthir eriron coch. Oet re rereint dan moꝛtuid gereint

105

garhirion graun wehin. Rution ruthir eririon gvīn.

Oet rerereint dan voꝛtuid gereint. garhirion grat

hit. turuſ goteith ar diffeith mẏnit. Oet re rereint.

dan voꝛtuid gereint garhirion gran anchvant. Blaur

blaen euraun inariant. Oet rerereint dan moꝛtuid.

gereint. garhirion.graun adaſ. Rution ruthir erẏrion

glas. Oet re rereint dan moꝛtuid gereint. garhiri⸗

on graun eu buẏd. Rution ruthir eririon llvid.

Ban aned gereint oet agoꝛed pirth new. rotei criſt

aarched prid mirein prẏdein wogoned.

GERAINT

Before Geraint,
the enemy of affliction,
I saw white horses
cowed down
and covered with blood.
And after raucous battle-cry
the kicking of daisies.

Before Geraint,
the enemy of pursuit,
I saw war-horses
cowed down
and covered with blood.
And after raucous battle-cry
plenty of time to think.

Before Geraint,
the enemy of oppression
I saw the white pelts
of horses.
And after raucous battle-cry
time to sleep easy.

At Llongborth didn't I see
sheer anger,
stretchers galore,
and bloodied men
before Geraint.

At Llongborth didn't I see
a mowing down,
men locked in struggle
with blood on their foreheads
before Geraint the great,
to his father a true son.

At Llongborth didn't I see
the digging of spurs,
men who would not flinch
before a spear,
and wine drunk
from shining glasses.

At Llongborth didn't I see
weapons, fighting men,
blood
oozing,
and after raucous battle-cry
came retreat.

At Llongborth didn't I see Arthur,
brave men
fighting with steel;
emperor,
marshall of effort.

At Llongborth wasn't Geraint killed,
and brave men
from the land of Devon,
even though they were killed
they did their share of killing.

Swiftly did they run under Geraint's thigh,
longlegs nurtured on wheat;
blood-stained in the onrush
like speckled eagles.

Swiftly did they run under Geraint's thigh,
longlegs nurtured on corn;
blood-stained in the onrush
like black eagles.

Swiftly did they run under Geraint's thigh,
longlegs devouring corn;
blood-stained in the onrush
like red eagles.

Swiftly did they run under Geraint's thigh,
longlegs eating mown corn;
blood-stained in the onrush
like white eagles.

Swiftly did they run under Geraint's thigh,
longlegs with a stag's leap;
the roar of a fire
on a mountain waste.

Swiftly did they run under Geraint's thigh,
longlegs greedy for corn;
the grey tips of their hair
like shining silver.

Swiftly did they run under Geraint's thigh,
longlegs fit for grain;
blood-stained in the onrush
like silver eagles.

Swiftly did they run under Geraint's thigh,
longlegs living on grain;
blood-stained in the onrush
like grey eagles.

When Geraint was born,
the gates of heaven
were opened.
Christ would grant
what would be asked of him:
you of fine form,
the glory of Britain.

Also published by
LLANERCH:

TALIESIN POEMS
translated by
Meirion Pennar

POEMS
John Dyer

THE HERBAL REMEDIES
OF THE PHYSICIANS
OF MYDDFAI
translated by
John Pughe

CELTIC FOLK-TALES
by F. M. Luzel

THE CELTIC LEGEND
OF THE BEYOND
by Anatole Le Braz

From booksellers.

For a complete list,
write to:
Llanerch Enterprises,
Felinfach, Lampeter,
Dyfed, SA48 8PJ.